Contents

Introduction

Snakes make surprisingly good pets. They are clean, quiet and easy to care for creatures that take up little space and do not need walks, grooming or vaccinations. Although not as cuddly as more traditional domestic pets, they are fascinating and low-maintenance animals.

This book will provide you with all the information you need to start keeping snakes. All the species are available in pet stores and suitable for the family or first-time keeper. The different species are organized in an ease-of-care order – the easiest to keep appear first, graduating to more demanding species.

Choosing a pet

Your own preferences and domestic situation will determine what types of snake are most suited to you and your family. You may want a small species, such as a Milk Snake, whose accommodation does not take up too much room, or you may select a larger species to handle regularly. Whichever you choose, you have to take responsibility for the snake's welfare throughout its life.

Space requirements

The size and shape of vivaria vary to suit different snakes and your choice will depend on the species, their age and the number of snakes to be housed. The following information gives an indication of space needed for each species.

Small: Milk Snake.

Medium: Corn, King, Garter, Rough Green, Children's Python, Brazilian Rainbow Boa, Yellow Rat, Bull (individuals only).

Large: Royal Python, colony of Garters, several Rough Greens, Boa Constrictor, Carpet Python.

Handling

Snakes become used to human contact within weeks of hatching or birth. Most species are very easy to handle and regular handling ensures that they stay tame. However, young people should only handle snakes under adult supervision.

Diet

All snakes are carnivores, but few snakes need to be fed live prey and all pet species should be weaned onto defrosted prey. Most of the species in this book eat rodents, but some eat fish or live insects. Snakes tend to be infrequent feeders, requiring a weekly or fortnightly feed.

When purchasing a snake ask for captive-bred juveniles that are proven defrost feeders. This will ensure that you start off with a fairly tame snake that has already been weaned onto dead food.

Where to obtain stock

Once you have decided to keep a snake it is essential to find a good source of livestock, and equipment and foods needed to keep it in good health. Visit specialist pet stores, rather than superstores, and speak to knowledgeable staff. Joining a herpetological society is also a good idea. To locate a good snake supplier look through pet care magazines, visit your local library and ask friends and parents. The internet is invaluable for anyone interested in herpetology (the study of reptiles and amphibians).

The Carpet Python has a much larger appetite than smaller species and it also needs big living quarters.

Selecting a healthy individual

If possible, choose a captive-bred animal that is feeding well. When selecting a snake, watch out for mites wandering around on its body – the snake will need treatment so do not buy it. The cylindrical body shape should otherwise have no noticeable bumps or lumps, which is a possible sign of broken ribs or a malformed spine. Do not be alarmed if baby snakes are presented to you in tiny boxes. They like small, secure spaces in which to establish themselves and to mature. Within several weeks your snake will be ready for its own vivarium.

Look for specimens:
- that are rounded but not bloated
- that have shiny scales and clear eyes
- that have a record card noting dates of feeding and sloughing, as well as the date of hatching or birth.

Avoid specimens:
- with a dirty cloacal area
- with sunken-looking eyes
- of a nervous disposition
- with bits of shed skin stuck to the body
- with red or pinkish belly scales, which may indicate an infection.

Captive-bred snakes

Juvenile captive-bred specimens make the best pets, simply because they have adapted to captivity and should not harbour any diseases or parasites. Some available species are not captive bred but are common enough in the wild to be acceptably harvested for the pet market.

Snake bites

Occasionally you may get bitten by your pet. It is unlikely to hurt much and should not put you off keeping snakes. A simple mistake of putting your hands close to a snake after you have been handling its food may trigger a bite and hold-on response. Should this ever happen, immerse your hand in a bucket of water and your snake will eventually let go.

Place the snake back in its vivarium and make sure you handle your pet again within a few days. Try to avoid a repeat

This is a healthy adult Yellow Rat, a popular medium-sized snake suitable for novice and experienced keepers.

performance, by washing your hands for example, and try to overcome any apprehension you feel towards your snake.

Home breeding

Pet snakes are usually kept and housed individually. Very few are social species that keep the company of other snakes, except for a short breeding or hibernation period. However, some species are so well adapted to captivity that if an adult pair are housed together under the right conditions they will eventually breed. Snakes either lay eggs (oviparous) or produce live young (ovoviparous). This book will not cover snake breeding, but herpetological societies will give excellent advice and more specific breeding manuals are available if you wish to pursue this topic.

KEY

In the species pages that follow each symbol shows the general care requirements and basic facts that will influence your choice of pet. This is general information only and more detailed requirements are given in the text.

Accommodation

This symbol indicates the type of housing each species requires. There are 3 basic types: arboreal, terrestrial and pet home.

Diet

Each snake's preferences are given under this symbol. All snakes are predatory carnivores. Most snakes eat only rodents, but some also like to eat small prey like fish or insects.

Maximum Life Span

Pet snakes will normally live longer than their wild counterparts and this information gives a rough idea of a pet's expected maximum life span in captivity.

Maximum Length

This information states the maximum length to which a snake will grow.

Baby snakes soon become accustomed to human contact.

Anatomy

Snakes are reptiles and, like mammals, are vertebrate animals that have a skull and backbone. They are classified into the order Squamata, and the suborder Serpentes or Ophidia. There are about 2,700 known species, which vary in size, diet, colouring and habitat. However, they are all basically cylindrical in shape and share common traits.

External Features

Ears

Snakes have no visible ears or eardrums, which means they cannot hear airborne sounds. This is because the bone that conducts noise from the eardrum to the inner ear is only connected to the jaw. This means that snakes can only sense vibrations at ground level.

Eyes

Snakes have fairly poor eyesight and only see the world in black and white. They lack eyelids, but their eyes are protected by a spectacle, which is a transparent eyelid scale that cannot be closed.

Tongue

All snakes have a long forked tongue. By slowly flicking the tongue up and down when extended, the snake picks up tiny particles from the ground or air. Once taken back into the mouth, these particles are analyzed by a structure in the roof of the mouth called a Jacobson's organ. This organ 'tastes' and 'smells' the environment.

Head

Eye

Skin

Snakes are covered in scales, which are hardened parts of the skin. These form a protective outer covering and prevent the snake from drying out (desiccation). Scales vary in size considerably; larger scales are usually found on the head and belly, and smaller ones appear along the body. Some species have keeled scales; that is, the scales have a ridge along the centre. When rubbed together these keeled scales may produce sounds.

Tail

Surprisingly, snakes do have tails. The length is measured from the cloaca (anal opening) to the tip of the tail end of the snake. As a general rule, males usually have longer and wider tails than females of the same species. The Boidae family also have two spurs next to the cloaca – the visible remnants of their ancestral limbs. Unlike some lizards, snakes never drop their tails for defence purposes.

Internal organs

A snake's body has many organs that are similar to those of mammals. They are somewhat elongated compared to that of a mammal, and the heart, liver, stomach and lungs are streamlined to fit the narrow body shape. All these organs are protected by a long ribcage.

Thermoregulation

Snakes are ectothermic, which means that they rely on their environment to warm or cool their bodies. Diurnal snakes (active in the daytime) seek warm rocks or sunlight to bask in order to stock up their energy levels. Once warmed, they can hunt and digest their prey. Unlike mammals, which consume food to maintain a steady body temperature, snakes use their food mainly to assist growth. Energy for movement is obtained largely from the environment.

To enable snakes to regulate their temperature properly the vivarium needs to have a gradient of temperatures. This enables snakes to thermoregulate at will by moving between cooler and warmer areas.

The term 'cold-blooded' also refers to ectothermic creatures, but it is misleading because a snake's blood may be hotter on a warm day than that of a mammal.

Body

Tail

Accommodation

It is essential to provide your pet snake with the correct environment – in terms of heat, light and space – in order to keep and maintain it successfully.

Snakes may be housed in very sparse vivaria, lined only with newspaper and a box for a retreat, as long as they are adequately warmed and have enough water, food and shelter. So long as the right conditions are created, a pet snake is unaware of how nice its home looks. However, most pet snake owners prefer a more attractive arrangement. You can be creative in decorating your snake's vivarium, but always ensure that the materials you use are not toxic or harmful to your pet.

Containers

A snake's home (vivarium) is most likely to be made out of the following materials:
Glass This is, in my opinion, the best and most attractive option for housing small- and medium-sized snakes. Glass vivaria can be purchased in a variety of sizes and shapes. Those with additional height are more important for climbing species, while vivaria with a large ground area are more suitable for terrestrial species. Glass is easy to clean but these vivaria must be adequately ventilated to ensure a constant supply of fresh air.

Plastic Pet homes are excellent for rearing baby snakes and for housing smaller species. They are cheap, colourful and well ventilated. They are particularly useful for feeding snakes away from their normal vivarium. However, they are not large or strong enough for a more powerful adult snake such as a boa or python. Heater

This cheap and hygienic type of accommodation is available in a range of sizes from most pet stores.

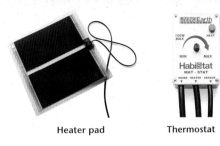

| Lighting options | Ceramic heater | Heater pad | Thermostat |

pads are the only suitable heating option for these containers.

Wood These vivaria have wooden sides and sliding glass doors at the front and they are strong, sturdy and easy to clean. Many sizes are available and some can even be purchased as a 'flat pack' for assembly at home. All the heating and lighting options available for snakes can be incorporated into this type of vivarium. Unless you have a spare room, most Boa Constrictors and large pythons will eventually need to be housed in this type of container.

The required dimensions of a vivarium are determined by the size of a snake, the numbers you are to keep together and their habitat requirements. Throughout this book vivarium dimensions are given as length x height x width.

Heating and lighting

All the snake species featured in this book require heating, and there are various pieces of equipment to provide the right sort of heat, as well as light, for your snake.

Heater pads Most pet snakes are warmed using heater pads. An excellent range of

low, medium and high wattage heater pads are available. Higher wattage pads need controlling with a thermostat. The pads need regular checking because their effectiveness can deteriorate over time. Remember, never cover more than half the ground area in the vivarium with a pad.

Light bulbs and spotlights These are very useful for providing direct heat and light to a basking area. Their other use is for background lighting so that you can see your snake more clearly. Animals and furnishings should be protected from contact with them, and these bulbs should be thermostatically controlled.

Ceramic heaters and infrared bulbs These are powerful heaters used for creating very hot basking areas within the vivarium. They must be thermostatically controlled and animals and keepers must be protected from contact with them.

Thermostat For proper temperature control within the vivarium, heaters and lights, except fluorescent tubes, should be regulated with an appropriate thermostat.

Thermometer All vivaria benefit from one or more thermometers to accurately measure temperature. They enable the keeper to monitor and maintain a temperature gradient within vivaria, which is needed by snakes to thermoregulate effectively.

Fluorescent light tubes This sort of light is beneficial for diurnal species and for general lighting purposes. No thermostatic control is required, since very little heat is emitted from these tubes.

When you buy heating and lighting equipment read fitting instructions carefully, and make sure that all electrical equipment is installed correctly by a capable adult.

Water

Water is essential for life and all the snakes in this book require fresh water. Ideally, sink a suitably-sized water dish into the substrate so that it can be accessed easily for drinking and bathing. Water should be checked and changed every other day, since some species are likely to bathe and then defecate in their water bowls.

Mist spraying is beneficial and helps to freshen up a vivarium and to keep the dust down. Even desert species, like Milk Snakes appreciate an occasional spray, but you should make sure that the substrate does not become damp. A pile of plastic plants, or moss, placed in an up-turned plastic box that are sprayed occasionally will create a humid micro-climate. This is likely to be

Hygrometer

used by most snakes from time to time, especially when they are due to shed their skins. A hygrometer can be used to measure humidity.

Substrates

A variety of materials, called substrates, are available to cover the base of a vivarium. Your choice is determined by the requirements of your snake and your aesthetic preferences. Snakes can be successfully kept on newspaper, but I prefer a more attractive and naturalistic looking display that incorporates a mixture of the following options.

Play sand and gravel These are useful for desert and burrowing species, such as Milk Snakes, which prefer fine rather than coarse sand.

Wood and bark chips These are the main substrates used by snake keepers and are available in 2 or 3 grades. Avoid the finest types because particles are likely to be taken in with foods, which can cause digestive problems.

Leaf litter Seasonal leaves, conkers, pine cones, etc., can all enhance the look of a vivarium. These are best frozen overnight to kill any resident pests. Leaf litter is ideal for Garters and Rough Green Snakes.

Reptile grass This green matting is easily washed and very versatile.

Paper It is easy to clean and replace.

| Wood chips | Leaves | Cork bark | Plastic plant |

Although snakes do not seem to mind a bare vivarium, it is always best to add a variety of materials into a snake's home to provide areas for exploration.

Shelters

Shelters and hiding places are essential for all snakes because they give a valuable sense of security. Natural cork logs and a range of manufactured shelters are available from pet stores. Toilet roll tubes and empty shoe boxes can also be used and are great for small snakes – simply throw the cardboard away once it is old or soiled. Snakes can never have too many shelters and care should be taken to make sure a snake can shelter in both the warm and cool parts of a vivarium.

Furnishings

Naturalistic backgrounds, real, plastic and silk plants, drift wood and cork bark can all be used to make your vivarium more attractive. Real plants are good for larger vivaria that also have full spectrum lighting. Plastic and silk plants are attractive and useful for providing cover,

resting and climbing areas. They can be washed and disinfected easily.

Set-ups

The basic requirements for a snake are a place to hide, somewhere to drink, and areas in which they can warm up and cool down. Most snakes have fairly similar housing requirements, but the size and shape of the vivarium depends on the size and type of snake.

Terrestrial

This vivarium provides a standard set-up and is suitable for most snakes that are kept as pets. Heater pads effectively warm the ground covering at one end of the vivarium and a small low-wattage bulb is available for light if and when required. This vivarium may be decorated in any way the keeper likes, providing the materials used are non-toxic and without sharp edges. The use of thermometers and a hygrometer are advised to monitor conditions inside the unit. Electrical equipment should be checked on a regular basis to ensure reliability.

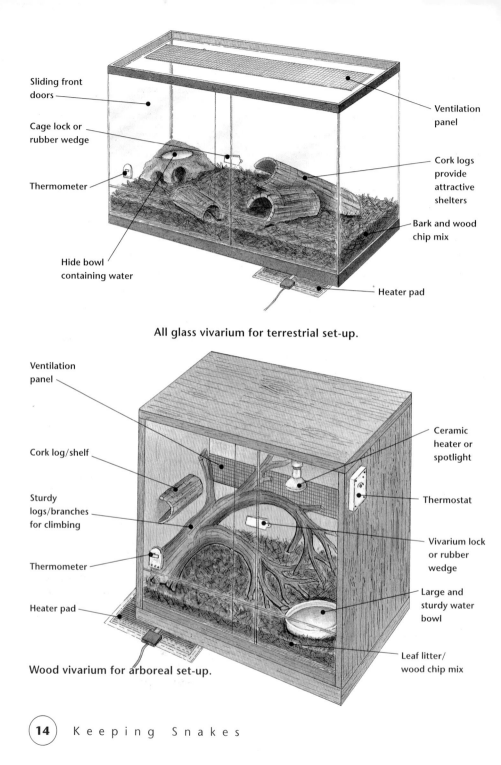

Sliding front doors

Cage lock or rubber wedge

Thermometer

Hide bowl containing water

Ventilation panel

Cork logs provide attractive shelters

Bark and wood chip mix

Heater pad

All glass vivarium for terrestrial set-up.

Ventilation panel

Cork log/shelf

Sturdy logs/branches for climbing

Thermometer

Heater pad

Ceramic heater or spotlight

Thermostat

Vivarium lock or rubber wedge

Large and sturdy water bowl

Leaf litter/ wood chip mix

Wood vivarium for arboreal set-up.

Arboreal

This set-up is suitable for climbing species, such as Carpet Pythons, Corn Snakes and Yellow Rat Snakes, as well as those species that are very active. It is ideal if several snakes are kept together, such as a group of Garters and Rough Greens. Essentially, this set-up combines plenty of opportunities for snakes to move about and rest off the ground, whilst still maintaining a good temperature gradient. Large species need sturdy branches and suitably-sized hiding places. The vivarium base may be decorated with bark chips and leaves or more plainly furnished with paper and a box. Providing the temperature and humidity are suitable, snakes are unconcerned about how their vivarium looks.

Pet Home

Most juveniles and smaller Milk Snakes will thrive in this type of accommodation because it is not too large to intimidate young snakes. Pet homes are not designed for use with powerful heaters and they do not have fixtures for spot lights or fluorescent tubes. Therefore, heater pads are used as the main heat source. Many sizes are available, but they are not secure enough for stronger snakes, which may push open the lids and escape. They are useful as feeding areas for those snakes fed outside their main accommodation. Plastic is a very safe material compared to glass, so a pet home may be the preferred choice of accommodation if a unit is to be set up in a child's bedroom or play area.

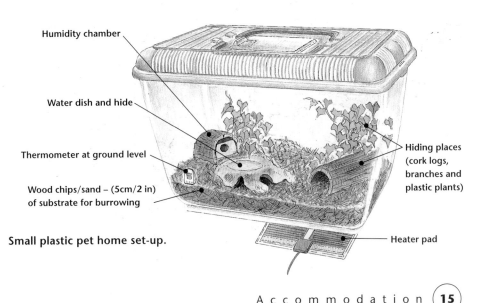

Humidity chamber

Water dish and hide

Thermometer at ground level

Wood chips/sand – (5cm/2 in) of substrate for burrowing

Hiding places (cork logs, branches and plastic plants)

Heater pad

Small plastic pet home set-up.

Feeding

All snakes need nourishing food to enable them to develop and grow. The amount and type of food they require will vary depending on their age, size and species.

Snakes are predators and will eat other animals. You can feed snakes almost any suitable prey. Fortunately, modern pet stores easily cater for a snake's feeding requirements. Using commercially farmed prey animals, rather than wild-caught ones, will guarantee your snake a regular supply of healthy and parasite-free foods.

- pup – hairless juvenile
- medium-sized rat
- large adult rat.

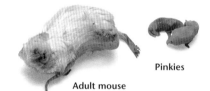

Pinkies

Adult mouse

Mammals

Mice (*Mus musculus*) Mice are the most widely used snake food. Pinkies are ideal for smaller snakes or juveniles of larger species. Mice come in three sizes:
- pinky – hairless juvenile
- fuzzy – haired juvenile
- adult – mature mouse.

Rats (*Rattus rattus*) Rats are ideal for larger snakes and it is easier to feed these species with one rat rather than several mice. They are available in three different sizes although rat pups are the most popular choice:

Rat

Rabbits (*Oryctolagus* species) These are available frozen in a range of sizes and are suitable for medium- to large-sized snakes.

Birds

Chicks and Chickens Commercially reared birds are widely available frozen, however, I personally think that they should not be the mainstay of a snake's diet because they lack the nutritional content of a rodent.

Fish

Frozen fish, such as smelt, are available from pet stores. The snakes in this book that eat fish live near freshwater habitats, so they should be fed freshwater fish, preferably whole, whenever possible.

Fish

Invertebrates

A range of live insects and other invertebrates are available to the keeper.

Crickets (*Gryllus* species) These are the most widely available insect food. A 'silent' form is available if you do not like the noise that loose ones can create.

Locusts (*Locusta migratoria, Schistocerca*

gregaria) These large, fat-bodied insects are suitable for most species.

Waxworms (*Galleria* species) Best offered to young snakes or those that are weak or stressed. Feed waxworms by hand or in a bowl to stop them from wriggling away into the corners of the vivarium.

Collecting your own

One problem of collecting your own food is the risk of introducing unwanted parasites, or insects affected by pesticides, into the vivarium. However, one benefit of using wild-caught insects and invertebrates, such as worms and spiders, is that they are full of naturally acquired vitamins and minerals.

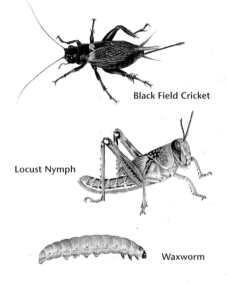

Black Field Cricket

Locust Nymph

Waxworm

(Illustrations not drawn to scale)

Processed Foods

Snake sausages These sausages are an alternative to rodents and are suitable for small- and medium-sized snakes. They have added vitamins and minerals, and some are specially formulated for individual species.

Garter grub This prepared food is ideal for many fish- and amphibian-eating species, which may miss out on some essential vitamins if fed solely on a diet of pre-killed fish.

Snake sausages   Garter grub

Dietary Supplements

Providing a snake eats regularly and its prey is healthy, there should be no need to supplement the diet with any extra vitamins and minerals. A snake obtains everything it needs from its whole food diet. The only real exceptions to this rule are fish- and insect-eating species, which benefit from some vitamin and mineral supplementation.

Feeding

Snakes eat their food whole. In the wild, small prey is often swallowed live while larger prey species, like rats, are suffocated by the tight squeezing coils of a snake's body. It is not necessary to feed live rodent prey to a pet snake in captivity unless, in rare instances, the snake will not eat anything else. After getting the snake to feed, you should wean it back onto a more acceptable diet of pre-killed food.

Most pet snakes are reared on whole dead foods from birth. The food should be stored in a freezer until required and then thawed out thoroughly before use – about one hour for a mouse. The food should then be placed in the vivarium/feeding container or offered to the snake with long tweezers. Never try to feed a snake slices of meat (raw or cooked) because they need the whole animal to ensure they remain in good health.

Feed your snake foods that are relative to its size. For example, start a juvenile Kingsnake on pinkies and graduate up to adult mice. Whilst a baby could not manage an adult mouse, an adult snake can still enjoy several pinkies as a change or a special treat.

Some snakes prefer to be fed either in the morning or evening. With some experience at judging behaviour you will soon recognize when your snake is hungry. They tend to be excited by any movement near the vivarium. Almost all snakes are ravenous after a shed but they are reluctant to feed just before shedding. Fresh water should always be available.

Avoid overfeeding your pet as obesity is the most common reason for visiting a vet for treatment.

Always remove uneaten foods from the vivarium and never re-freeze defrosted foods. It is important to prepare and store foods under hygienic conditions. If you do decide to keep and breed rodents, make sure that you keep and kill them in a humane way.

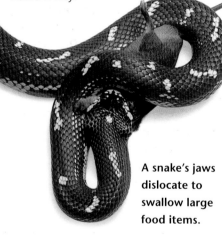

A snake's jaws dislocate to swallow large food items.

Feeding hints and tips

I would suggest feeding your pet snake in a different container, away from its living quarters. In this way it should not automatically assume that food is on offer whenever the vivarium is opened. It will become used to being handled or moved prior to a meal, minimizing the risk of a bite due to fingers being mistaken for a tasty food morsel.

Once settled into their new home most snakes should not pose any real problems with their feeding habits. Sometimes a bit of variety in the diet helps if a snake appears bored of its usual foods. If you think you have a problem try some of the following:

• Offer your snake food using a pair of long tweezers – gently try to interest the snake in eating by dragging the food around the vivarium/feeding container. Once keen and ready to eat, leave the food alone and withdraw slowly from the feeding container to allow your snake to feed in private. Patience and persistence may be necessary for a while with a particularly difficult feeder.

• Leave nervous snakes undisturbed when they are feeding – they are often quite secretive in the wild.

• Some snakes prefer to feed overnight, or under reduced light conditions, so leave food for them at these times.

• A well-fed snake may fast or refuse food for a few weeks or even months. Providing the snake is otherwise in good health this is quite normal behaviour and you should not be unduly alarmed.

• Check the vivarium temperature and humidity levels to make sure that it is not too hot or cold, too dry or damp?

Californian Kingsnake

Lampropeltis getulus californiae

Terrestrial

Mammals/Birds

10 –15 years

120cm (48in)

Kingsnakes are an American species and are native to the region from Canada in the north to Ecuador in South America. They live in a range of habitats, from pine forests to desert, dry riverbeds to mountain slopes. They may also be found in suburbs of cities, school playgrounds, waste ground, and in parks and gardens.

In the wild, Kingsnakes are aggressive predators eating a range of prey – lizards, birds, rodents and other snakes. They are called Kingsnakes because they will actively catch, kill and eat other snakes, even highly venomous ones. For this reason this 'king of snakes' is tolerated in back yards and gardens in areas where dangerous snakes may be found.

Thousands of Kingsnakes are bred every year by hobbyists. They are ideal pets because they tend to enjoy being handled, prefer small, secure vivaria and rarely suffer from a loss of appetite. These medium-sized snakes grow to a length of about 120cm (48in) and live for approximately 10-15 years in captivity.

Whilst most Californian Kingsnakes appear banded with black and white hoops, striped forms are also available. More Kingsnakes are being selectively bred in captivity and their markings now vary considerably, from jet black to chocolate brown, brilliant white to creamy yellow.

Several closely related species (subspecies) exist and these snakes can be cared for in the same way as a Californian Kingsnake. Each

SIMILAR SPECIES

Florida King
Lampropeltis getulus floridana

•

Mexican Black King
Lampropeltis getulus nigritus

•

Speckled King
Lampropeltis getulus holbrooki

A snake's skin is shiny but never slimy.

Black and white banding is only one of the patterns found on this species of snake.

Snakes 'taste' or 'smell' their environment using a forked tongue.

Round pupils are characteristic of snakes that are more active during daylight hours.

subspecies has different patterns and colours, so they are worth looking out for. All Kingsnakes are ophiophagos, which means they will eat each other as well as other snakes. For this reason they must be kept separately, even as juveniles, or you risk losing one of your pets. A clean, dry vivarium measuring 90 x 30 x 30cm (36 x 12 x 12in) is more than adequate for a single adult. A temperature gradient ranging from 26.5-32°C (80-90°F) at the warmest end and 24°C (75°F) at the cooler end is ideal. Kingsnakes are a terrestrial species and

Kingsnakes make ideal pets because they are friendly, enjoy being handled, prefer small secure spaces and rarely lose their appetite.

because they are not great climbers, furnishings should include a base substrate of paper, bark chips, leaf litter or a mixture of the above. Adding rocks and cork bark can help to create an attractive display.

Water should always be available and regularly changed. Most snakes will not drink every day but they should have the option of a fresh drink at all times. Occasional mist spraying and the inclusion of a humidity box are beneficial.

Make sure your Kingsnake is fairly tame and a regular feeder before purchasing one from a dealer or breeder. The very youngest snakes are initially very snappy; they strike out and rapidly vibrate their tails as a threat/defence posture – they have yet to learn that you mean no harm. The best course of action is to handle your juvenile a few times a week. It will soon realize that you are not a threat, especially if you offer it an occasional food reward. Kingsnakes soon tame and will rarely offend their keeper by biting.

These snakes tend to feed well and their dietary needs are satisfied by a diet of dead rodents. All they need for a healthy life is the domestic mouse in their diet.

Without overfeeding them, offer your

Mexican Black Kingsnake

Banana and chocolate Californian Kingsnake

Florida Kingsnake

Many subspecies of Kingsnake are available in a variety of patterns and colour combinations.

Observation Point

Eyes

The eye itself is one of the few distinguishing parts of a snake's anatomy and not surprisingly most snakes have evolved some means of camouflaging the eye so that it is not easily spotted by other animals. An eye stripe is a popular method of disguise and is favoured by snakes such as the Royal Python, Brazilian Rainbow Boa and Boa Constrictor.

The eye is always open to the light. A transparent scale, or spectacle, covers the eye protecting it from dust and other foreign bodies. When a snake is ready to slough the spectacle appears milky blue, clearing just before the actual shedding process begins.

Compared with most reptiles, snakes have relatively good vision and by examining their eye shapes, herpetologists can make educated guesses regarding a snake's habits.

Round pupils These are found in snakes that are active during daylight hours (diurnal). Snakes, such as Garters and Kingsnakes have round pupils.

Vertical pupils Nocturnal species, and those that are active at dusk or before dawn (crepuscular), often have vertical pupils. The pupil expands in near darkness to catch all available light. Children's Pythons have these pupils.

Horizontal pupils These are rare in snakes and normally found only in arboreal species that need to judge distances during climbing.

Look at the eyes of your snake, or others in this book, to discover their hunting habits. Also, notice how the eye changes when your snake is ready to shed its skin.

pet as much as it can eat in approximately 10 minutes, every 6-8 days. Don't worry if your pet eats erratically. Most snakes eat very regularly for some time and then will refuse food for a while. Also, most snakes are very hungry after a slough but may refuse food just beforehand.

Kingsnakes, unlike most constrictors, are able to kill more than one animal at the same time. A Kingsnake finding a nest of rodents, for example, can kill one by mouth and hold and crush others within its coils, or against the ground. This is rarely seen in pet snakes feeding on dead food, but offer your snake two dead mice at once and see what happens.

Sinaloan Milk Snake

Lampropeltis triangulum sinaloae

Pet Home

Mammals

15 years

1m (3.2ft)

Milk Snakes are the smaller and more colourful members of the Kingsnake group. There are 25 recognised subspecies, all technically starting with the Latin name *Lampropeltis triangulum*. They are widely available from snake breeders and good pet stores. Most species are also small and easy to rear and breed.

Sinaloans can grow up to 1m (39in), but they are usually much smaller – on average 70-80cm (27.5-31.5in). They are frequently referred to as tri-coloured milks because they have the typical tri-coloured bands of black, white and red along the length of their bodies. The red or orange bands are particularly wide in this slim Mexican species. Milk Snakes also have a typically small snout.

In the wild Milk Snakes inhabit the same habitats as Kingsnakes, but their range extends just a bit further north and south in the

A ribcage extending along the length of the body helps the snake to grip the ground.

Milk Snakes tame quickly and are easy to handle.

Extremely vivid colours contribute to the Sinaloan's popularity as a pet.

Americas. Milk snakes vary in size considerably – those living in the north of the range tend to be smaller than their relatives from warmer countries in South America.

Wild Milk Snakes are generally crepuscular or nocturnal, but in the safety and warmth of your home they may be active at any time. However, they prefer to spend much of their time in secure hiding places. Wild Milk Snakes catch and eat small prey, such as lizards, rodents and even other Milk Snakes; for this reason it is recommended that individuals are homed separately.

All Milk Snakes require the same type of care, but larger species will need larger accommodation. The Sinaloan is best kept in a small, secure vivarium measuring 60 x 30 x 30cm (24 x 12 x 12in). The vivarium should be warmed from below to establish a temperature gradient, maintaining the hottest parts at 30°C (86°F) and the cooler end at 21-23°C (70-74°F). All Milk Snakes prefer a good depth of substrate with no heavy objects, such as

Milk Snakes are known as tri-colours because of the coloured bands on their bodies.

SIMILAR SPECIES

Pueblan Milk Snake
Lampropeltis triangulum campbelli

•

Mexican Milk Snake
Lampropeltis triangulum anulata

•

Pueblan Milk Snake
Lampropeltis triangulum hondurensis

rocks, which may crush them as they hide amongst and move about the substrate. Leaf litter, bark and wood chips, and cork pieces are ideal. They like a dry environment and so only a small water dish is required. Add a small humidity chamber to help your snake when shedding. A good secure purpose-built vivarium is essential for this snake because they are slight in build and very good at escaping.

Sinaloans rarely have problems feeding but they tend to prefer several smaller items to one very large one, so pinkies are ideal. Milk Snakes eat as often as Kingsnakes, so feed your pet for about 10 minutes every 6-8 days. Make sure that no substrates are eaten with their meals.

They can be a bit jerky in their movements when handled initially, but they tame relatively easily and over time become easy to handle. They may bite, but since they have a tiny mouth a nip will do little harm.

Corn Snake

Elaphe guttata guttata

Arboreal

Mammals/Birds

10-15 years

1.5m (5ft)

Corn Snakes, also known as Red Rat Snakes, are attractive and colourful snakes that are native to the warmer parts of the USA. They have a good temperament, feed well and are easy to breed in captivity. For these reasons they are amongst the most sought after species for both novice and experienced keepers.

Corns are named after the cornfields and corn stores in which they search for rodent prey. Great climbers and burrowers, they can scale up tree trunks or root about under straw or hay with equal skill. Their natural colouring consists of burnt orange blotches or orange saddles, ringed in black over a tangerine background. The belly scales are often black and white chequers. As a result of captive breeding many colour varieties are available. Juvenile Corns may be purchased with names such as Black Corn, Snow Corns or Zig Zag, which refer to their colouring.

Medium-sized snakes will

These snakes are active climbers and their attractive markings offer effective camouflage.

Corn Snakes are an attractive species with a good temperament, making them a popular choice with snake keepers.

measure between 80-150cm (31.5-60in) and they will live for 10-15 years in captivity. They usually breed from approximately 2 years to 6 years of age, which is their natural lifespan in the wild.

Corn Snakes require a warm and dry vivarium with an average temperature range of 25-30°C (77-86°F) in the summer, cooling slightly in winter to 20°C (66°F). An adult pair need a vivarium measuring 90 x 60 x 60cm (36 x 24 x 24in). Newly hatched snakes and juveniles need to feel more secure and safe so they need much smaller housing. Units measuring 24 x 10 x 10cm (9.5 x 4 x 4in) and 60 x 30 x 30cm (24 x 12 x 12in) respectively are ideal. Decor should be thoroughly cleaned before placing in a vivarium; especially substrates such as leaf litter, which may introduce unwanted pests. Overnight freezing of leaves will ensure that most pests like mites or ticks are killed. Logs, stones, cork logs, leaf litter, bark chips, climbing branches can all be used for decoration and will provide

The orange markings are called saddles because they lie across the top of the body.

Warm and dry surroundings help to keep the scales in good condition.

SIMILAR SPECIES

Prairie Rat Snake
Elaphe guttata emoryi

•

Black Rat Snake
Elaphe obsoleta obsoleta

Most snakes prefer small, 'secure' accommodation. Big, open spaces tend to make them feel nervous.

plenty of climbing areas and secure retreats for your pet.

A shallow dish filled with water should be available at all times. Corns also appreciate regular mist spraying almost as much as a humidity chamber. Humidity chambers are an invaluable aid to improving the quality of life and the comfort of your snake. As you gain experience in keeping snakes, you will recognize how dry or humid a vivarium is and will be able to maintain a good balance between too little and too much humidity (air moisture).

Corn Snakes feed well and juveniles may be offered several pinkies or furries every 7-10 days. Adults will require 2-3 adult mice every 2 weeks. However, they are not robots and their feeding requirements do vary. Be flexible when feeding Corn Snakes and try to avoid over-indulging this species as they rarely refuse a feed.

Regular handling when a Corn Snake is still a baby will help it to understand that humans mean no harm. Indeed, your snake will soon realize that humans are a good source of warmth and food. Babies initially strike out at anything that

approaches, but once they are handled and fed regularly they should calm down and begin to relax. It is at this stage, at around two months of age, when they are feeding regularly on dead pinkies, that they are ready to leave a breeder or pet store to go to a new home. Remember only buy juveniles that are relatively tame and feeding regularly.

If not handled regularly, most snakes can be easily shocked when your hand starts searching the vivarium. Some snakes may strike out and bite as a means of defence or in expectation of food. Firm deliberate actions, such as reaching straight in and lifting the bulk of the snake,

This species requires access to fresh water and enjoys regular mist spraying and an occasional bath.

Observation Point

Sloughing

As snakes grow, they periodically shed or moult their outer layer of skin. This process is called ecdysis. The faster a snake grows the more frequently it will shed its skin. Juveniles grow very quickly, so they shed more often than mature snakes. Some adult snakes shed only once or twice a year, whereas baby snakes may go through ecdysis every 6 weeks or so.

A few days prior to shedding a snakes' colours will appear dull and the spectacle covering the eye will cloud over. In order to loosen the old skin and start peeling it back, a snake will rub its snout along a rough surface, such as stones or a branch. With writhing body movements that press against objects the skin will gradually peel off and is left inside out trailing behind the snake.

Sitting in a humidity chamber will help the snake moisten and lubricate the skin and assist it in the process of sloughing. Some snakes sit in their water bowls at this stage. Most snakes, even very large ones, can shed their skin in one long, unbroken piece. Occasionally, a spectacle or other bits of skin may be stuck and left behind. To remove the remaining bits of skin, spray the snake liberally with water and carefully peel off the remaining skin using a pair of tweezers. If you find that the skin doesn't shed regularly in one piece, it may be due to low humidity in the vivarium. This should be corrected to prevent further problems for the snake.

is a good approach to minimize this problem. Snakes prefer being approached from front rather than top opening vivaria. To a snake there is something particularly threatening about sudden predatory movements from above. Corn Snakes are not difficult to handle, but they are agile and can soon slip inside a sofa or under a floorboard, so keep a good eye on your pet and do not lose it or let it escape!

Yellow Rat Snake

Elaphe obsoleta quadrivittata

Arboreal

Mammals/Birds

15 years

1.8m (5.9ft)

This snake is native to America, and is found in parts of Florida, Georgia and Carolina. It is often associated with and found near water, canals, human habitation, barns and wood stores.

The Yellow Rat Snake is variable in colour, from yellow to orange, and is characterized by stripes running from behind the head along the full length of the body. Juveniles tend to have blotchy markings but they gradually acquire adult markings as they mature. Hatchlings, 30cm (12in) in length, lack the distinctive stripes seen on adults. Their patchy pattern fades as they mature into adults.

These are large snakes and adults are capable of reaching 2.1m (7ft) or more. However, they still prefer quite small accommodation – a vivarium measuring 120 x 45 x 45cm (48 x 18 x 18in) would suit a pair.

This is a typically yellow, Yellow Rat Snake; some specimens are orange in colour.

This species is a close relative of the Corn Snake and just as easy to keep in captivity.

SIMILAR SPECIES

Baird's Rat Snake
Elaphe bairdi

The temperature range should be between 25-30°C (77-86°F). Whilst most pet snakes are maintained at steady temperatures year round some, like the Yellow Rat Snake, benefit from a cooler winter period lasting a few weeks. A suitable temperature would be 21°C (70°F) since this is neither too hot nor too cold for the snake to rest in.

Juvenile Rats lack the stripes that are visible on mature snakes.

These snakes are frequently kept and bred by herpetologists in very small and plain breeding units consisting of paper as a substrate, a hide box and water bowl. However, if you only have one or two snakes to look after, you may want to set up a more attractive and naturalistic looking vivarium. Leaf litter, bark chips, smooth gravel and mosses are all suitable substrates. Sturdy climbing branches are also useful inclusions since this snake likes to investigate its surroundings. This climbing snake enjoys some height, so make sure to include elevated logs or a shelf for it to rest on and hide in. As long as this snake is warm and can hide, it will remain unaffected by the simplicity or effort taken in decorating its vivarium.

Often referred to as chicken snakes in the USA, adults will consume a variety of prey, including chicks, chicken eggs, bats, mice and other rodents, such as small rabbits. However, as pets they are happy to eat pinkies and mice.

These are greedy snakes and they are unlikely to become difficult to feed. Appetites vary from individual to individual, but as a general guide feed adult snakes 4-5 adult mice every 2 weeks. Juveniles should be offered several pinkies or furies every 7-10 days, according to size. Occasionally your snake may want more, or less, and sometimes it will refuse food altogether.

Baby Rat Snakes are very wild initially but they soon tame, which makes them a popular snake for handling. They enjoy hiding, especially in pockets where they can peep out every now and then. However, remember that most snakes should not be handled for several days just after a feed. Some do not mind, but others prefer to be left alone to digest their food.

Royal Python

Python regius

Terrestrial

Mammals/Birds

20 years

2m (6.5ft)

Native to West African grasslands and forest clearings Royal Pythons are solitary terrestrial creatures frequently inhabiting mammal burrows. In the wild, they mainly hunt at night and during the early hours of morning and evening (crepuscular).

This attractive species is an excellent choice of pet. They can reach a maximum length of 2m (6.5ft), but they are usually much smaller at 1m (3.3ft). However, they are never too large to become unmanageable and have a great temperament. In Africa they are often called the 'shame' snake due to their lack of fierceness. If disturbed or nervous, a Royal Python curls up into a ball with its head buried under its coils. This behaviour is rarely seen in captivity as they adapt readily and happily to life as a pet.

An adult or several juvenile pythons require a vivarium

Heat sensitive pits between the scales on the upper lip allow Royals to 'see' infra-red images of prey.

measuring 120 x 45 x 45cm (48 x 18 x 18in). To begin with, a baby Royal Python may prefer a much smaller pet home. Snakes feel more secure in small spaces, at least initially. Once they begin to grow and settle in they will not mind a larger vivarium. Several Royal Pythons can be kept together, but if kept alone they will not become lonely.

Blotchy patterns help to camouflage this python in the wild.

Royals are the best choice for a pet python, since they are mild mannered and just the right size for handling.

SIMILAR SPECIES

Children's Python
Liasis childreni

•

Carpet Python
Morelia spilota variegata

•

Burmese Python
Python molurus

Royals enjoy fresh air so the vivarium should be well ventilated and heated within a 24-29.5°C (75-85°F) range. These snakes really enjoy their shelters and will frequently lay coiled within a cork log or similar bit of vivarium furnishing with just their head sticking out to enable them to watch their surroundings.

A base substrate of newspaper is fine, but wood or bark chips are much more attractive. Leaf litter also enhances the appearance of a vivarium. As a terrestrial species height is of little importance, but Royals will climb up and rest on top of cork logs or other shelters to bask. A spotlight or ceramic heater controlled by a thermostat may be required to heat a larger vivarium; however, in a warm house heater pads should be sufficient.

Most reptiles, including pythons, enjoy an occasional bath. Mist spraying every so often is recommended and a humidity chamber placed within the vivarium should help prevent dehydration and ensure regular skin shedding.

Pythons are clean animals, only going to the toilet every 10-14 days. Cleaning is therefore kept to a minimum and soiled areas are easily removed. Occasionally snakes will defecate in their water bowl. This will need thorough cleaning before being replaced with fresh water and should be sited away from any heat sources.

A juvenile Royal should be offered foods, such as mice, about every 6-12 days, and adults every 10-14 days. Once well fed these snakes are likely to refuse food, or fast, for a period of time, ranging from a couple of weeks to several months. There is no need to be unduly alarmed. Pythons lead relatively inactive lives and have simply become full. In time, particularly after their next slough, feeding will resume. If in doubt about your python's

A close-up of the Royal Python's skin shows the beautiful skin patterns and how the scales overlap one another.

health, consult a herpetologist. They will probably confirm that your pet has had plenty to eat and is otherwise in good health. Should you be concerned that your snake is actually sick, consult a herptile-familiar veterinarian. A record of its feeding habits would be useful in any diagnosis.

Royal Pythons are easy to handle but make sure that you support most of their body – do not let them dangle or jerk them around. Most snakes wrap around you when being handled – smaller ones on the

This captive-bred juvenile is just the right size to go to its new home. It is also ready to be handled on a regular basis.

Observation Point

Is my snake male or female?

Sexual differences are often clearly visible in animals. However, with many snakes you may need to make careful observations before you can actually deduce whether they are male or female. Many juvenile snakes are best sexed once they are between 8-12 months old. It is at this stage that they have become more developed and are on the verge of adulthood. Looking at two, or more, similar-sized snakes will also make the differences much more apparent.

Things to look for:

Body size Males tend to be more slender than females.

Tail length Tails are much longer in males. Female tails tend to taper off quickly after the cloaca (anal opening). The bulge at the top of a male's tail

(after the cloaca) is its hemi-penis, which is a twinned reproductive organ. In boids (pythons and boas) the cloacal spurs are noticeably longer and more obvious in males.

MALE

FEMALE

The bulging area after the cloaca is a sure sign of a male. They definitely have more sub-caudal scales (those found underneath the tail) than females of the same species.

hand, wrist and fingers, larger ones on the arms and neck. If your snake is wrapping itself too tightly around your body or won't let go, reach for its tail. Once you have a snake by its tail you are effectively in control and can easily unwrap it; it is much safer than tugging at the middle of its body. Royal Pythons are too small to cause any real concern unless handled by a very young child. In general, however, Royals are one of the friendliest of snakes and make an excellent choice of pet.

Common Garter Snake

Thamnophis sirtalis

Terrestrial

Mammals/
Invertebrates/Fish

8-10 years

1.2m (4ft)

Garter Snakes are native to North and Central America and many of those that are kept as pets come from Canada. They thrive in captivity – even wild-caught snakes can, with gentle handling, tame in a very short period of time. Once Garters realize that you are not a predator but a provider of warmth and food, they start to enjoy their time in your hands.

Common Garter Snakes are slim and active. They are beautifully marked with creamy lines and reddish flanks. In the wild they hunt in aquatic environments and will eat fish and amphibians, such as tree frogs and tadpoles. In captivity they are generally fed on dead fish.

There are over 50 types of Garter Snake and all of them can be kept under similar conditions.

In the wild, Garter Snakes are active diurnal hunters of small animal prey such as tadpoles and frogs.

An adult pair require a vivarium measuring at least 120 x 38 x 38cm (48 x 15 x 15in). Juveniles should be reared in much smaller containers measuring 48 x 30 x 18cm (19 x 12 x 7in).

This terrestrial species prefers a dry vivarium equipped with a large water bowl and substrates such as wood chips, leaf litter, coir or peat. Logs, branches and living ferns may also be included, which offers your snake plenty of spaces for

Long, slender and fast, this species is an agile and accomplished swimmer.

The keeled scales make Garters feel rougher than other species.

Heater pads are excellent for keeping snakes warm, especially at ground level. However, remember that heater pads should only be used at one end of the vivarium. To encourage breeding the vivarium temperature should drop over the winter months to around 10°C (50°F).

Many keepers remove their snakes to another container at feeding time. They should be fed separately if several snakes live together because they have a tendency to fight over food. When two snakes attack the same morsel, one may end up eating the prey as well as the other snake. Garters should also be provided with large water bowls. They really enjoy the exercise they get in a shallow bath and, if fed

This is a beautifully-marked snake, with creamy white lines and reddish flanks.

exploration and secure hiding places. A humidity chamber is essential to ensure good skin conditioning. The substrate should be kept warm using a heater pad and a temperature range established at 20-26°C (68-79°F) for much of the year. If spot lamps are used for overhead heating, they should be controlled using a thermostat and the temperature gradient should be monitored with a thermometer.

SIMILAR SPECIES

Aquatic Garter Snake
Thamnophis couchi

•

Blue-striped Garter Snake
Thamnophis sirtalis sirtalis

outside of their main vivarium, they are likely to feed and then defecate in the same place. This eases the cleaning routine of their main vivarium. Some snakes become ill from consuming substrates that become attached to their food, so feeding in another container should help overcome this problem.

Initially, feed your snake whatever it will eat in 10-15 minutes, 2-3 times a week. Once it is well fed, the amount eaten per sitting will reduce and sometimes food may be refused. Garter Snakes mainly feed on defrosted fish. To begin with it is often best to wriggle the food about a bit using a pair of long tweezers. Once your snake recognizes this as live food you can start placing the fish in a shallow water dish to help stimulate a feeding response. Small rodents, such as pinkies, and earthworms are also likely to be taken by many Garter Snakes. In the wild, Garter Snakes eat only live foods. In captivity, if they are exclusively fed a diet of dead fish, thawed from frozen, there is a good chance that the snake will suffer from a deficiency of an important vitamin called Thiamine. To avoid this you should vary

A simple plastic container is ideal to make a humidity chamber, such as the one shown here.

their diet. So long as your Garter eats some worms, pinkies or garter grub, a processed snake food, this problem should not occur.

As Garters eat regularly they need a good hygiene regime, so soiled substrate should be removed and replaced on a regular basis. Keeping your snakes clean helps to keep them healthy.

Garter Snakes generally handle very well. Only very nervous individuals may defecate on you, but this is rare and usually only happens once or twice whilst a juvenile or wild caught snake is going through the first steps of taming. Wrapped around your fingers, a snake will enjoy being stroked under the chin.

This snake has a clouded eye and is shortly due to shed its skin. Placing the snake in a humidity chamber will assist in this process.

Observation Point

Hibernation/aestivation

At certain times of the year many snakes, such as Garters, find the weather too cold to find food, remain active and to escape from predators. To avoid death, these snakes retreat underground, into hollow logs or other areas protected from freezing temperatures. Huddled together in groups or alone, snakes reduce their metabolism to conserve energy during this resting period, which may last for many months. No food or water is taken in and body functions, such as shedding and digestion, stop altogether. This process is called hibernation. The onset of warmer weather gradually stirs the snakes into action. Upon emerging they will usually shed their skin and become very interested in finding a mate, food and water – usually in that order. Most snakes then disperse, setting off on their own, only regrouping with other snakes the following winter.

In some tropical countries snakes behave in a similar way, but in this instance they avoid hot rather than cold weather. They retreat into cool caves or deep into hollowed out tree trunks. In tropical areas this rest period is called aestivation.

Pet snakes do not need to hibernate/aestivate, but some may rest for a period of time – their heating mechanism can be reduced or switched off for a period of a few weeks. Care must always be taken to make sure ectotherms (animals that require an external heat source to maintain body temperature) do not get too hot or too cold. Keep them in a frost-free area away from other pets or pests.

Many snakes only get into a breeding condition during this hibernation or cooling period. As they emerge in spring, many snakes from temperate climates breed and the birth of baby snakes usually coincides with the birth of their prey. In tropical climates a short cooling period is still often required but the breeding response and arrival of new prey usually coincides with the arrival of a rainy or wet season.

If you intend to try to rest or hibernate a snake allow it to digest its last meal and gradually cool it down. Regularly check to make sure that your snake is not experiencing problems.

Rough Green Snake

Opheodrys aestivus

Arboreal

Invertebrates

8-10 years

90cm (36in)

The Rough Green Snake is a small and very gentle species that is usually found in the vicinity of streams, lakes, canals or ponds. It is grass green in colour and, unusually for a snake, it is insectivorous. These snakes are native to the eastern USA, with a range from New Jersey to Florida, and westwards to Texas, Kansas and into northern Mexico.

These snakes possess large round pupils and are diurnal, which means they actively hunt their spider and insect prey in the daytime. Bright green when viewed from above and a creamy yellow colour below, these semi-arboreal snakes are superbly camouflaged and effectively disappear when they climb amongst bushes, shrubs, twigs and branches.

The Rough Green can grow to approximately 90cm (36in) in

length but it does have smaller, more terrestrial, relatives in the USA. The Smooth Green Snake *Opheodrys vernalis* reaches between 38-51cm (15-20in) in length, while an Asian relative from Taiwan grows to 102cm

These beautiful, delicate looking snakes are a social species and may be kept in small groups in an arboreal set-up.

(40in) and eats mainly earthworms.

Rough Greens are widely available in the wild, so little effort has been made to captive breed them on a regular basis. They are legally collected and exported under a strict monitoring system and during the writing of this book there have been no major concerns about keeping these snakes.

These are not the easiest of snakes to find at specialist pet stores but this species is well worth asking about and waiting for. They can be kept in groups or on their own, and may share a community vivarium with other similar sized but non-cannibalistic species, such as Garter Snakes. They enjoy temperatures in the range of 23-25°C (74-77°F), which is easily established with heater pads or a combination of heater pad and spotlight bulb controlled by a thermostat. In winter this species can rest, cooled down for several weeks in a box of leaf litter and moss at about 10°C (50°F). This cooling is essential to encourage breeding in this particular species.

Long and slender, this species is an agile hunter of invertebrates.

Rough Green Snakes have lengthened tails, which are used for gripping and balance.

Keeled scales give the Rough Green its roughness.

They should be housed in a vivarium measuring at least 90 x 38 x 38 cm (36 x 15 x 15in). House your Rough Green in a dry but regularly mist-sprayed vivarium; they do not like the damp but thrive in a small amount of humidity. By decorating your pet's home with some mosses, a 5cm (2in) depth of leaf litter and incorporating a humidity chamber, you will provide for all their essential needs. As they

Experts in the art of camouflage, Rough Green Snakes can suddenly 'disappear' amongst green and twiggy foliage.

are a lightweight snake, fine branches, twigs and even house plants will give them something suitable to climb on. A low ultra-violet output pet tube should also be included in the vivarium to maintain your pet's health.

One of the things people like most about Rough Green Snakes is that they do not need to be fed rodents and are happy to exist on a diet of spiders and insects. In the wild, they will also occasionally consume small lizards and frogs, so I would advise a varied diet when possible. They are fascinating to watch as they stalk a big fat juicy cricket or grasshopper. You can try almost any available live insect foods. However, try to limit the number of mealworms because these are less palatable and less nutritious than crickets, which are also widely available. Smooth non-hairy caterpillars are relished and grubs like waxmoth larvae are worth offering to your pet. Spiders should be caught only if you are certain that they are not poisonous. Rough Greens are unlikely to eat dead foods, but try

Easy snakes to tame, this Rough Green is happily wrapped around the warm hand of its owner.

Observation Point

Each type of scale found on a snake has a different name (*see below*).

Scales

All snakes have scales, which are thickened pieces of the outer layer of skin. They are made out of a hard substance called keratin that is also found in hair and feathers. Each species has a different patterning of scales and many of them have larger scales on the head – often called shields. Scales may be counted as guides to identify a species or to determine the sex of a snake. Many scales have a ridge along their length called a keel. In some species these can be rubbed together or vibrated to make a noise. They also give snakes a better grip, which can easily be felt in the hand. The Rough Green Snake has these keeled scales – look carefully to see the ridge along the scales.

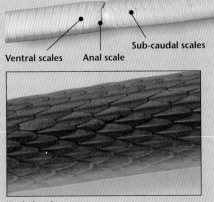

Ventral scales   Anal scale   Sub-caudal scales

Keeled scales

See if you can locate all these different scales, and then maybe draw them. Try to locate them on a shed skin too. Compare the size, shape and number of scales. Generally, male snakes have more sub-caudal scales than females.

offering pinkies – it is an option worth trying because they are very nutritious.

Feed your Rough Green as much as it will consume at one sitting, several times a week. Some live foods should also be available in the vivarium for ad hoc feeding. This snake's health will also benefit from the addition of ultra-violet drops or supplements added to its food.

As its name suggests, this species has rough, or keeled, scales and it does not slide through the fingers like so many smooth-scaled snakes. They are, however, simple to handle and tame easily. Delicate as well as dextrous, these climbing snakes have a very investigative nature.

Children's Python

Liasis childreni

Terrestrial

Mammals/Birds

20 years

1m (3.2ft)

Essentially a small and secretive snake, the Children's Python is native to most of northern Australia but absent from the extreme south of the country. Like many pythons, this species is very adaptable and is likely to be found in coastal forests as well as inland deserts, preferring to rest in termite mounds, under rock overhangs or other small hiding places.

A dark brown stripe behind the eye helps to camouflage this light brown, blotchy-patterned python. Underneath, the wide belly scales are usually a creamy white colour.

Like most pythons, this species requires a warm and dry environment. Temperatures should be maintained within the range 23-30°C (74-86°F) because a bad chill could be life

This species enjoys living and hiding in small spaces.

A stripe behind the eyes helps to camouflage this earthy-coloured snake.

Small pythons, such as this species, are easier to handle and are more suitable as pets than their much larger relatives.

Like all pythons, this species of snake lays eggs.

make sure you position them carefully so as not to injure your snake should the rocks topple over. Line the base of the vivarium with a substrate of cork and wood chips.

In the wild Children's Pythons feed on any small mammal, bird, frog or lizard they are able to catch. As pets they are usually excellent feeders and take readily to their diet of mice or small rats. A few small mice offered every 10-16 days or so should be enough to satisfy their needs.

Never growing too large or becoming awkward to handle, this species has a good temperament. They are generally very passive and suitable for regular handling. Like all small snakes, the Children's Python needs careful supervision when handled. Preferring small, secure hiding places these snakes have a habit of disappearing into holes in chairs and sofas and it may be some time before they decide to come out!

threatening. It is therefore essential that thermometers and thermostats are used to maintain adequate but not excessive warmth. A combination of 'hot' rocks and heater pads may be considered and this nocturnal snake has no need for ultra-violet or other overhead lighting.

A 90 x 38 x 38cm (36 x 15 x 15in) vivarium is adequate for this small snake. Should you choose to keep your python in a larger vivarium, make sure that there are plenty of small hiding places available to give your pet the sense of security it requires; most snakes prefer places they can squeeze into rather than a big cave. Use rocks to create an attractive, naturalistic vivarium display. However,

SIMILAR SPECIES

Royal Python
Python regius

•

Carpet Python
Morelia spilota variegata

Brazilian Rainbow Boa

Epicrates cenchria cenchria

Arboreal

Mammals/Birds

15-20 years

1.9m (6.2ft)

The iridescent scales of this boa give it its name. Like oil on water the skin displays a vivid spectrum of colours that shimmer and change depending on the light and your angle of vision.

The scales have microscopic ridges that act like prisms – refracting sunlight to give a stunning show of colour. All boas do this to some extent, but it is very pronounced in this species. Photographs never really show the effect as seen by the naked eye.

The underlying colour is basically of a reddish-brown hue, with rings and spots along the entire length of the body. The shades of colour are very variable and the spots and rings tend to fade as the snake matures.

Rainbow Boas are common in many regions of South America, including Brazil, Guyana and much of the Amazon basin. They inhabit a wide range of habitats, ranging from rainforest to grassy plains and scrubland. This snake grows

Rainbow Boas enjoy climbing aided by their 'gripping' tail.

Heat sensitive pits are characteristic of 'sit-and-wait' or ambush feeders.

A good temperament and vivid, shimmering markings make the Brazilian Rainbow Boa a popular choice of pet.

to an average length of 1.22-1.52m (4-5ft) but some may grow to 1.9m (6.2ft).

These boas are simple to keep and tame easily. They can be housed communally but are usually housed satisfactorily in separate vivariums. They

This species, like all Boas, produces live young regularly in captivity.

require a warm, dry vivarium with a temperature range of 22-30°C (72-86°F). Some humidity is needed but the vivarium should never be damp. A 90 x 38 x 38cm (36 x 15 x 15in) cage should be fine for an average specimen, otherwise use one measuring 120 x 38 x 38cm (48 x 15 x 15in) for a larger one. An occasional mist spray is sufficient to keep the vivarium atmosphere fresh and just right. A substrate mixture of mosses, wood and bark chips arranged to a depth of 5cm (2in) or more should be provided.

Rainbow Boas are lazy snakes that prefer to wait and ambush their meals rather than having to chase their dinner. This species,

like all boas, is naturally inclined to feed on birds and mammals, and the dextrous long jaws open to consume surprisingly large prey. The heat sensitive pits situated on the mouth give the snake's brain a thermal image of its warm-blooded prey, so it may help to warm up it's food to give the snake a better image of its meal. Feed your boa as much as it can eat at one sitting, every 7-10 days. Most Rainbow Boas are kept, and even bred, on an exclusive rodent diet. Take care not to overfeed them – you will soon notice when a good feeder starts to put on weight.

This species is naturally nocturnal in the wild, but captive-bred individuals are active whenever they feel like it. Like all boas, they give birth to living young and are a relatively easy species to attempt breeding should your interest for these snakes grow.

Rainbow Boas are easy to handle but should be well supported when held in the hand. They may be handled at any time, and have gained a reputation for being a pleasant and popular snake.

Bull Snake

Pituophis melanoleucus sayi

Terrestrial

Mammals/Birds

16 years

2.2-2.7m
(7-9ft)

Bull snakes are large and powerful predators feeding almost exclusively on small mammals. Although they can reach over 2.1m (7ft) in length, 1.5m (5ft) is a more average size. Highly variable in patterning and colouring, they are one of America's most attractive snakes. Fifteen subspecies are known and are found ranging from southern Canada right down into Central America. Depending on locality, they are commonly called Bull, Pine or Gopher Snakes. Bull Snakes are called Gopher Snakes in the USA because they eat large amounts of burrowing mammals called gophers.

Bull Snakes are very popular with cereal farmers in America and apparently they are still caught from the wild, and even purchased, for

The patterning and colouring of Bull Snakes is highly variable.

Northern Pine Snake
Pituophis melanoleucus melanoleucus

release into granaries and barns where they are very effective at eating rats, mice and squirrels.

Bull Snakes are noted for the noises they make and their violent defence posturing. An irritated or threatened Bull Snake inhales a large amount of air,

swelling itself to make it appear larger than it really is. Also, by opening its mouth, posing in a typically serpentine 's' shaped posture and appearing to strike up towards its real or imagined foe, it gives the impression of a formidable opponent. But, like most snakes, even venomous ones, it is largely bluff and the snake would prefer to make a hasty retreat rather than have a violent confrontation.

Surprisingly, most snakes in the world are silent and unable to hiss at all. However, Bull Snakes have a special membrane, or skin flap, in their windpipe and when this is vibrated by exhaled air it

Using a scale on their snout and loops of the body, this species can 'dig out' rodent prey from their burrows.

If disturbed or attacked, Bull Snakes will grunt or snort like a bull.

makes a loud hissing/rasping sound. The name Bull Snake comes from the sound large specimens can make, which is similar to that of a bull snorting and grunting.

A large vivarium measuring 180 x 60 x 60cm (72 x 24 x 24in) is ideal for an adult or breeding pair. Bull Snakes are secretive

Bull Snakes have an enormous appetite. They are rarely difficult to feed and will accept most types of food.

The raised scale or point on a Bull Snake's snout is used for digging and burrowing.

but quite active and like a warm and dry vivarium with some height to enable them to climb. They also enjoy burrowing under substrate such as paper or wood chips. Do not use finer substrate, such as sand, since this can irritate a snake's skin – chunkier pieces like moss, bark chips or plain paper are best. A temperature range of 24-27°C (75-80°F) is adequate and under-floor heating, using heater pads to warm the substrate, is recommended.

A spot lamp may be used to create a basking area but this must be controlled using a thermostat to avoid overheating the vivarium.

Water should be available at all times although this snake is not known for its love of bathing. It will, however, appreciate occasional mist spraying. Remember not to

Wide, smooth ventral (belly) scales, provide snakes with a good grip to allow forward movement.

Observation Point

Mating and breeding

The silent male snake is attracted to a female by her 'smell' – a chemical, or pheromone, trail that she leaves for the male to follow.

If you do attempt breeding, notice how excited a male snake becomes in the company of a female of the same species. The tongue flicks in and out more frequently, sometimes rapidly, at other times staying extended in long, slow and rhythmic movements. At this time the snake is 'distracted' and will not be interested in feeding, for example. His body movements become jerky, twitching in a state of heightened awareness prior to mating. Watch how the snakes stroke one another, the male rubbing his chin along the female's body and rubbing against her. Their bodies eventually entwine during mating.

Providing mating has been successful the gestation period begins and, depending on the species, lasts between 1-6 months. Most snakes lay eggs but some, particularly those from cooler habitats, give birth to live young. Live-bearing snakes featured in this book include boas and garters.

Bull snakes are egg layers, with a gestation period of about 40 days. If your pet snake successfully mates you will need to provide a suitable area for laying the eggs – usually a covered, vermiculite and moss filled box, into which the female will bury the eggs.

Parental care is virtually unknown and snakes fend for themselves from birth onwards. In the wild, there is a very high death rate whereas in captivity most snakes will survive to adulthood.

over-spray since this snake is happiest in a semi-arid, desert or dry-forest-type habitat.

A Bull Snake should be fed as much as it will eat every 7-10 days. Mice, rats and other rodents are all accepted. They are unlikely to refuse any suitably-sized mammal or bird.

Juvenile captive-bred specimens are worth waiting for since they have already adapted to life in the vivarium and are used to being handled. As they grow the physical strength of these snakes becomes apparent. They are already quite a handful at only 60cm (24in). These snakes are fine to handle, but they are very strong and so should not be handled by a small child.

Carpet Python

Morelia spilota variegata

Arboreal

Mammals/Birds

30 years

5m (16.5ft)

This very attractive medium-sized python is common throughout much of Australia and New Guinea. They are particularly common around barns and other man-made agricultural buildings, attracted by the scent of rodents such as mice, rats or rabbits. They reach a maximum length of 5m (16.5ft); however, they usually grow to a length of 2m (6.6ft).

Carpet Pythons are accomplished climbers but they are also an extremely adaptable species of snake. They may be found in arid desert-like environments living on mammals and also high in rainforest canopies using their prehensile tail for extra climbing dexterity, hunting tree-dwelling prey.

Their markings vary greatly, ranging from black and grey with blotches and stripes to a deep yellow or rusty colour. Their name is thought to come from the 'oriental carpet' look of the

SIMILAR SPECIES

Diamond Python
Morelia spilota spilota

This is a fairly large species of snake only suitable for the more experienced keeper that has adequate space.

patterns on their bodies. The closely related subspecies Diamond Python *Morelia spilota spilota* is patterned with diamond-like marks – hence its name – and grows to about 2.5-3m (8-10ft), although specimens over 3m (14ft) exist.

The Carpet Python should be housed separately. It requires a large dry vivarium and the temperature should be maintained at 23-30°C (74-86°F). Cover the vivarium base in paper or wood chips rather than with sand or fine materials and add ground and elevated shelters. Good climbing branches need to be sited at a safe distance from any light bulbs or ceramic heaters used to heat larger vivariums. A heater pad, or two, placed on the ground should keep even the largest cages warm.

Initially, juveniles should be housed in vivariums measuring 90 x 45 x 45cm (36 x 18 x 18in). As they mature, Carpet Pythons should be housed in larger cages or

The fairly dark-colouring of this species is excellent for camouflage in the wild.

Clearly visible heat-sensitive pits detect and locate prey.

enclosures measuring approximately 180 x 60 x 60cm (72 x 24 x 24in), which is adequate for medium-sized specimens. If possible, vivariums should be larger than this and many people construct their own. Good ventilation is always important but draughts must be avoided since pythons like to keep snug and warm.

This popular pet is an impressive snake that will readily eat any bird or mammal offered. My own specimen, a 3.5m (11.6ft) male, is captive bred and a good defrost feeder. He is rarely handled, only every month or so, usually when the vivarium is soiled or needs a good clean. He is very tame and now has progressed to eating rats, as he is much too big to bother with mice. Feed juveniles several mice every 7-10 days. Offer sub-adults 2 rats every 7-10 days and adults should be offered 2-3 medium rats every 2 weeks. The amount eaten will vary depending on size and appetite, but Carpet Pythons enjoy food and are more likely to be plump than skinny.

This is a close-up detail of the Carpet Python's patterns and colouring. Their markings vary greatly.

Some Carpet Pythons will bathe regularly and others will only do so rarely or never. Always offer your python a water bowl, preferably quite a large one, even though they may rarely use it.

These snakes are quite amenable to handling, but larger snakes are never as relaxing to hold as the smaller King, Milk or Corn Snakes. Very few large snakes are content to settle down on your lap. These snakes tend to move about or coil themselves a bit too tightly around nearby objects rather than settle down calmly. Also do not forget that they can be quite heavy. Many snake keepers prefer to watch their behaviour within the vivarium.

Carpet Pythons are a large species of snake that require careful handling because they are fairly restless and heavy.

Observation Point

Feeding

Most snakes are opportunist feeders and have no set method of killing prey. Smaller, defenceless animals, such a frogs or young rodents are simply eaten alive. Prey that can fight or bite back is normally constricted until it is asphyxiated.

The jaws of snakes are very flexible and with their elastically expandable lower jaw most species can consume surprisingly large food items. Prey is held by the teeth and pulled into the mouth. Food is always swallowed whole and usually headfirst. The process of digestion begins almost immediately and snakes can speed up digestion by warming themselves, particularly around the belly area. Over the next few days or week, depending on the size of prey, a snake will defecate. Snakes defecate irregularly, usually following their last meal eaten approximately 10 days previously.

Look out for a snake's yawn – it opens and stretches its mouth when it is about to resettle the mouth joints after eating. Also, time your snake's feeding and note the time between eating a meal and the next time it defecates.

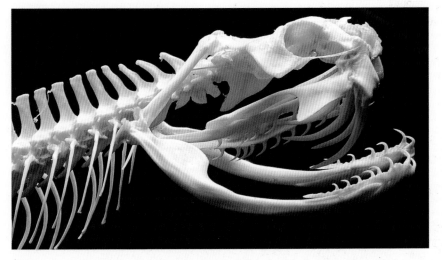

Only venomous snakes have fangs, clearly visible in this Gaboon Viper skeleton.

Boa Constrictor

Boa constrictor constrictor

Terrestrial

Mammals/Birds

20 years

4m (13.2ft)

Of the larger snakes, Boa Constrictors are the most frequently kept and bred species in captivity. They have been particularly popular in the Americas because their geographic range extends from Mexico in the north and southward though most of South America.

Despite their media image, which shows them attacking jungle explorers and poisoning large beasts, Boa Constrictors are non venomous and rather placid. These nocturnal creatures prefer to remain hidden during the daytime in old mammal burrows, hollow logs or camouflaged amongst the leaf litter.

Boas have an unusual skin texture. When you touch them, they feel more fabric-like that scaly. They have a basic creamy-grey coloration with diamond-shaped patterns and a peppering of spots. Whilst the colouring of boas is very variable amongst the 11 recognized subspecies, they are normally very attractive and remain a very popular snake.

Boa Constrictors are heavy bodied and can range from between 2-4m (6.5-13ft) in length, although 2.7-3m (9-10ft) is a more common adult size. They are good climbers, feeding readily on mammals and birds in the wild.

Make sure you really are capable of caring for and housing such a snake before purchase – as a Boa Constrictor grows it will require larger food items and eventually a big vivarium.

Juveniles can be housed in a 60 x 45 x 45cm (24 x 18 x 18in) or 90 x 45 x 45cm (36 x 18 x 18in) vivarium, however, adults will require a larger cage or enclosure measuring at least 2m (6.6ft) square. A Boa Constrictor requires a spacious and dry home warmed within a range of 25-32°C (77-90°F) to provide the comfort it

Brazilian Rainbow Boa
Epicrates cenchria cenchria

•

Red-tailed Boa
Boa constrictor ortonii

requires. Only sturdy climbing shelves or branches are suitable for such a chunky snake. Cork logs are ideal for offering a sense of security, but boas are quite happy to sit out in full view most of the time. Any substrate will suit this species but avoid sand and the finer grades of wood or bark chip. A large water bowl is welcomed and this species will bathe occasionally, often for many hours or days at a time. Mist spray occasionally to freshen up the environment. Good ventilation is important but draughts must be avoided.

Boa Constrictors have long and sharp, backward pointing teeth. These are particularly useful for grasping and holding onto feathered prey that could struggle and escape from less well-designed teeth. Many people assume that Boa Constrictors kill their prey by bone constricting. However, boas, like many snakes, grasp

This species loves bathing and regular mist spraying with a plant sprayer.

A boa's skin texture is unusual – it is more like soft material than scaly to the touch.

This is a medium-sized, heavy bodied snake that is a popular pet species for the experienced keeper.

Boa Constrictor (57)

Boa Constrictors have mottled belly, or ventral, scales. This is an unusual feature in snakes.

their prey by the head and squeeze it. The prey is stunned by the initial strike and dies from heart and lung failure – not from crushed bones.

With such long teeth and a powerful bite, boas are best kept and handled under adult supervision, even though most well tamed and cared for boas will never bite. A bite from one of these larger snakes will certainly require some first aid attention. Boas are large snakes and should be handled with care. Larger specimens may need two or more people to lift them. Tame specimens pose few problems but an aggressive large boa requires firm and careful handling.

To transport a snake, all but the smallest should be placed in a cloth bag, pillow or duvet and tied securely at the top. Smaller snakes can be transported in their pet

homes. However, make sure snakes do not chill when being moved.

Like all larger snakes, boas are best fed with caution. Prey should be dropped onto the floor or wiggled on long tweezers for younger specimens that have not yet adjusted to taking static and dead food. Always ready to accept mice, rats or small rabbits they can also occasionally be fed on chicks and young chickens. Feeding your pet with smaller prey in greater quantities may be more efficient if you wish to handle your snake regularly – the smaller items are more quickly digested and make handling more comfortable for the boa. One of the main benefits of having a defrost feeding regime is that snakes are tamer and less likely to be alert to any movement representing a possible food source. They

Boa Constrictors possess colours and patterns that enable them to blend effectively into their surroundings.

Observation Point

Camouflage patterns and bright colours

Most snakes have colours or patterns that enable them to blend in with their surroundings. Browns, greys and green colours are very typical of well-camouflaged snakes, especially tree-dwelling species. Blotches and stripes are also quite effective for a snake wishing to remain out of sight, especially in long grass or under a tree in dappled sunlight. Some snakes have quite bright colours and patterns that are also very efficient camouflage on a leaf-strewn floor in a tropical rainforest.

Many baby snakes have a different pattern as hatchlings than they do as adults. These markings are probably a more effective disguise for babies and less effective for adult snakes.

Many other snakes, such as King and Milk Snakes are so brightly coloured that they are in effect advertising themselves for all to see. There are two possible reasons why these snakes have evolved with such bright colours:

- They wish to startle a predator to give themselves time to escape.
- Their colours have evolved to resemble venomous snakes, in the hope that predators will confuse them with poisonous snakes and hence not attack them.

What purpose does your snake's patterns and colours serve? Are they purely for camouflage purposes or can you think of any other reasons that patterns and colours help snakes survive in the wild?

Draw your snake, photograph it against different backgrounds to note the effects – do they camouflage well? Also notice the skin colour fade before a shed and the brightness of the skin just afterwards.

become conditioned to expect dead and static items to eat and are much less likely to bite or strike out.

As a general rule, juveniles and adults should be fed as much as they can eat at least every 7-10 days. Feed small mice to young snakes, adult mice for larger, immature snakes, and rats or small rabbits for adults. Occasionally, when your snake is well fed, it will refuse food for several days or weeks. Do not worry because this is normal reptilian behaviour.

Record Card

A record card should hold as much information as possible about your snake. It is by recording observations and measurements that snake enthusiasts (herpetologists) learn more about these amazing reptiles.

Snakes are difficult to follow and study in the wild, so very little is known about their lifespans and natural behaviour. Observing and making notes will help you to discover more about their habits. For example, record what, and how often, your snake eats. Keep and measure shed skins, and record the date your snake sheds.

It is a good idea to draw, paint or photograph your snake. All snakes have slightly different colours or markings, so once recorded you can easily identify it from any other snake.

If your pet becomes ill, it may help you or your veterinarian to treat it properly if you have a record of its life history. A record card is also a useful source of information for anyone else who has to care for your pet whilst you are away.

Here are some of the things you may wish to record:

- Common name and scientific name
- Hatch date or birth date
- Length
- Food eaten or refused
- Details of skin shedding, when and how successfully
- Toilet habits
- Temperature range of vivarium
- Hibernation details or length of fasts

Fascinating facts may be discovered by keeping notes on your pet's development.

Record Card

Species   Male/Female

Name   Age

Hatch date   Preferred foods

Length

Date	Time	Event	Notes
e.g. for a Royal Python			
1 June	7pm	Fed	2 pinkies eaten very greedily.
16 June	6pm	Moult	Started to shed today. Sprayed it with water and watched for 20 minutes as skin sloughed completely.
17 June	10am	Fed	Snake very hungry – it had 4 pinkies this morning.

Snake Quiz

How well do you know your snake?

Test your knowledge with the quiz below.

1. Which popular snake curls up into a ball for defence?

2. Do snakes have legs?

3. What do terrestrial snakes do?

4. Do snakes have a heart?

5. What is a predator?

6. Do snakes chew their food or break it into pieces?

7. What is the longest snake in the world?

8. What does crepuscular mean?

9. Boa Constrictors are ovoviviparous snakes. What does this mean?

10. Are all snakes ectotherms?

11. Carpet Pythons have a prehensile tail. What do they do with it?

Answers

1. The Royal Python *Python regius* (its American name, the Ball Python, is derived from this characteristic). 2. No. However, some snakes, such as pythons and boas, have remnants of ancient limbs called spurs that are located by the anus. 3. They live on the ground rather than living above ground in trees and branches (arboreal snakes). 4. Yes. 5. It is a carnivorous animal, which means it hunts and eats other animals. 6. Neither, snakes swallow their food whole. 7. The Reticulated Python *Python reticulatus*. 8. It describes animals that are active at dawn or dusk, or in low light. 9. It means that they give birth to live young. 10. Yes. They rely on external heat to maintain their body temperature. 11. They use it a) to grasp and wrap around objects, b) to make a noise and c) as a deadly weapon.

Useful Information

There are many societies and clubs that you can join. They are an excellent source of information about the maintenance of herptiles (reptiles and amphibians) and all aspects of natural history. They are also a good way of contacting like-minded individuals and obtaining livestock.

Societies

British Herpetological Society
c/o The Zoological Society of London
Regent's Park
London NW1 4RY, UK.
To receive more information, write to the above address enclosing a stamped addressed envelope.

International Herpetological Society
Secretary: Mr K. J. Hingley
22 Busheyfields Road
Russells Hall, Dudley
West Midlands ·DY1 2LP, UK.
Membership by subscription. Monthly newsletter and quarterly journal entitled *The Herptile*. Lots of local branches.

Clubs

The Ark Pet Club
PO Box 150, Middx, TW8 8RF
arkpetclub@animal-ark.co.uk
Members receive colour newsletters on the care of pets. Regular articles and advice available by e-mail. Write or e-mail for details.

Pets on the Brain
www.petsonthebrain.com
An e-commerce pet site. You can read articles and e-mail questions regarding the care of reptiles and/or purchase reptile products.

Magazines

Pet Reptile
Freestyle Publications Ltd
Alexander House, Ling Road, Tower Park
Poole, Dorset BH12 4NZ, UK.
E-mail: petreptile@freepubs.co.uk
A monthly publication available from newsagents.

Reptilia
Muntaner 88, 5.1
08011 Barcelona, Spain.
www.reptilia.net
A colour bi-monthly magazine available on subscription or at specialist outlets.

Vivarium
Vivarium Publishing Group
PO Box 300067, Escondido, CA 92030, USA.
www.thevivarium.com
Published 6 times a year and available on subscription or at specialist pet stores. This is one of the best publications currently available.

Suppliers

King's Reptile World
35 Parkway
London NW1 7PN, UK.
www.kingsreptileworld.co.uk
A specialist reptile outlet specializing in captive-bred species.

The Vivarium
55 Boundary Road
London E17 8NQ, UK.
www.thevivarium.co.uk
A long-established herpetological store, specializing in captive-bred species.

Index